Symbolville

MIRROR LAND

SHAPE CITY

TENS PLACE

EXIT
NUMBERLAND

population 123,456,789

ALICE IN NUMBERLAND

FANTASY MATH

TIME LIFE *for* Children ®

ALEXANDRIA, VIRGINIA

ALL ABOUT I LOVE MATH

The *I Love Math* series shows children that math is all around them in everything they do. It can be found at the grocery store, at a soccer game, in the kitchen, at the zoo, even in their own bodies. As you collect this series, each book will fill in another piece of your child's world, showing how math is a natural part of everyday activities.

What Is Math?

Math is much more than manipulating numbers; the goal of math education today is to help children become problem solvers. This means teaching kids to observe the world around them by looking for patterns and relationships, estimating, measuring, comparing, and using reasoning skills. From an early age, children do this naturally. They divide up cookies to share with friends, recognize shapes in pizza, measure how tall they have grown, or match colors and patterns as they dress themselves. Young children love math. But when math only takes the form of abstract formulas on worksheets, children begin to dislike it. The *I Love Math* series is designed to keep math natural and appealing.

I have something to do with the number 10! Guess what it is. Then look at page 38.

How Do Children Learn Math?

Research has shown that children learn best by doing. Therefore, *I Love Math* is a hands-on, interactive learning experience. The math concepts are woven into stories in which entertaining characters invite your child to help them solve math challenges. Activities reinforce the concepts, and parent notes offer ways you and your child can have more fun with this program.

We have worked closely with math educators to include in these books a full range of math skills. As the series progresses, repetition of these skills in different formats will help your child master the basics of mathematical thinking.

What Will You Find in *Fantasy Math*?

In *Fantasy Math* your child will join Alice and her bird Max as they journey through Numberland, a magical place filled with all sorts of mathematical challenges. Along the way they will learn how a baker divides a birthday cake into equal parts for some unexpected guests, decipher the way a friendly dragon talks about numbers, and compare the nearly identical homes of twin gnomes. To help Alice find her way back home, your child will answer special Riddle Rabbit questions about the numbers 4, 7, 10, 12, 16, and 21.

Be sure to refer to the map on the inside cover of the book as you and your child "travel" through Numberland. Help your child figure out where Alice would be on the map as you begin each story. And don't forget to look for Alice throughout the book. She may be hiding but if you look closely, you'll find her!

After you've experienced *Fantasy Math,* we're certain you and your child will join Alice in saying:

I LOVE MATH!

The Editors
Time-Life for Children

Rub-a-dub dub. We're filling a tub. To find out why turn to page 12.

Table of Contents

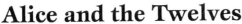

1 2 3 4 5 6 7

ALICE IN NUMBERLAND

"Ouch!" said Alice as she fell into the tulips.

"Ouch yourself!" said a voice. "Do I know you?"

"Well, I'm Alice and this is my bird, Max. Who are you and where am I?" she asked.

"I'm Number Card Four and you're on my foot," the voice said.

"Oh, I'm so sorry! Excuse me," said Alice as she scrambled to her feet.

MATH FOCUS: SPATIAL SENSE AND NUMBERS. Children learn about the number 4 while listening to a talking Number Card.

Have your child turn to the map of Numberland at the beginning of the book and find Alice. Have your child trace the polka-dot road with his or her finger. Then discuss Numberland and its 5 regions.

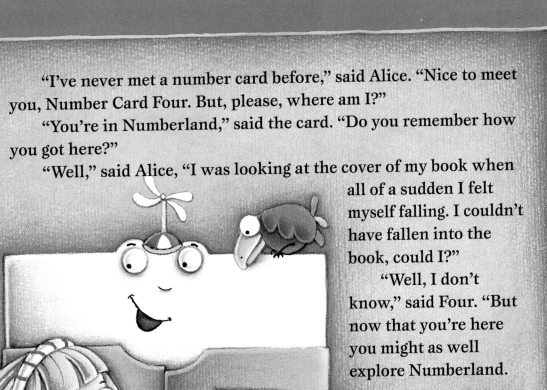

"I've never met a number card before," said Alice. "Nice to meet you, Number Card Four. But, please, where am I?"

"You're in Numberland," said the card. "Do you remember how you got here?"

"Well," said Alice, "I was looking at the cover of my book when all of a sudden I felt myself falling. I couldn't have fallen into the book, could I?"

"Well, I don't know," said Four. "But now that you're here you might as well explore Numberland.

It's a wonderful place full of fun and surprises."

MORE FUN. Have your child look for all the sets of "fours" in this story, such as 4 buttons, 4 pockets, 4 tulips.

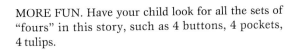

"I would like to stay for a while, but I really must be home in time for dinner. How can I get back home?" asked Alice.

"You get back by going ahead," said the card. "You must follow the polka-dot road until you find an exit. If you travel along every page in this book you're sure to find your way out. There is just one little catch."

"Uh-oh!" said Alice.

"It's part of the fun, really. Let me explain. As you make your way along the polka-dot road, you will pass through amazing lands filled with mathematical marvels and surprises."

"Oooh," said Alice. "What sort of surprises?"

"Well, from time to time, you will meet up with a riddle rabbit!" Four replied. "You must answer all its questions, puzzles, and riddles before you can move on through Numberland."

"What's a riddle rabbit?" asked Max as he flew onto Alice's shoulder.

"Why, I have one right here!" Four exclaimed, and he pulled a rather rectangular rabbit from his cap. "Number cards always have riddle rabbits with them," he went on. "So whenever you meet a number card, you'll find a riddle rabbit waiting for you."

Alice watched as the rabbit grew and grew and grew until it was all she could see.

"Ready to begin?" asked Four, and they stepped onto the next page.

I am the minute hand from this watch. When I show the same time as this digital clock, what number should I point to?

Alice
AND THE
FOURS

What am I?

I am one of the months of the year.
I have 30 days.
My first day is silly.
I am the fourth month.

Which coin am I?

?

You need 4 of me to make a dollar.

What comes next?

MATH FOCUS: TIME, MONEY, HEIGHT, ADDITION, AND SUBTRACTION. By exploring the number 4 in several different areas of mathematics, children interpret the many uses of numbers encountered in the real world.

As your child answers the riddles, discuss how each one uses the number 4. At 4 o'clock, show your child the time on an analog clock and on a digital clock.

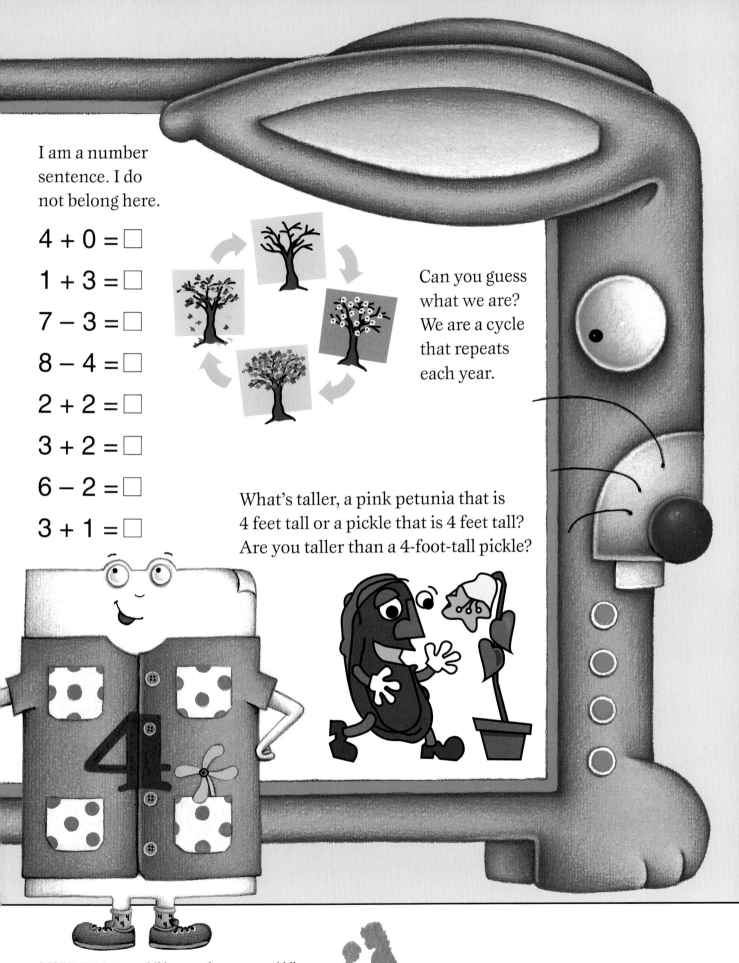

I am a number sentence. I do not belong here.

4 + 0 = ☐
1 + 3 = ☐
7 − 3 = ☐
8 − 4 = ☐
2 + 2 = ☐
3 + 2 = ☐
6 − 2 = ☐
3 + 1 = ☐

Can you guess what we are? We are a cycle that repeats each year.

What's taller, a pink petunia that is 4 feet tall or a pickle that is 4 feet tall? Are you taller than a 4-foot-tall pickle?

MORE FUN. Your child can make up some riddles involving the number 4 and challenge family members to solve them.

Alice hadn't gone 3 steps when she heard someone crying. Being curious, she went to see who it was.

FILL 'ER UP!

In addition to being wonderful rulers, the king and queen of Math-a-lot were incredible inventors. They were always tinkering around in the palace and making improvements.

One day, King Inchandfoot and Queen Yardly took Prince Fillup and Prince MT down to the moat to give them their yearly bath. The boys cried and thrashed unhappily.

"Goodness, I wish there was an easier way of doing this," said King Inchandfoot as he scrubbed behind Fillup's ear.

"So do I," complained the queen. "This water is so cold! I'd bathe them in a kettle if I could."

"That's it!" said the king. "What a good idea!"

The king and queen wrapped towels around the chattering princes and went off to the royal workroom. In no time at all, the king and queen had their contraption ready.

MATH FOCUS: ESTIMATION AND CAPACITY. By exploring several ways to fill a bathtub, children gain an understanding of the capacity of different containers.

12

Have your child find Math-a-lot on the map of Numberland. Help your child figure out that the larger the containers, the fewer are needed to fill the bathtub.

"Children, come here and see what your father and I just made," called the queen.

"Wow! What is it?" wondered Prince MT as he examined a huge copper kettle perched near the wide fireplace by the outside wall.

"It's for bathing," explained the king. "Now you can bathe all the time, and in warm water."

"I'm all for that," said Prince Fillup. "Can we try it?"

"Yes, but first we have to fill it with water," said the queen.

Each prince grabbed a teaspoon from the workbench. "We'll be right back," they said.

The princes ran to the moat and filled their spoons with water. They walked back carefully, being sure not to spill a single drop. When they reached the royal workroom, they each emptied one teaspoon of water into the bathtub.

Plop! Plop!

About how many teaspoons of water do you think it would take to fill the contraption? About 10? About 100? About 1,000? More?

Can you think of a better way to get the water from the moat to the bathtub?

MORE FUN. Your child can place 5 teaspoons of water in a cup, estimate how many teaspoons of water are needed to fill the cup, and then fill the cup with the teaspoon to check. Your child can also use a gallon container to see how many gallons it takes to fill your bathtub.

"Hmm," said the queen. "At this rate it will take you about a week to put in enough water for a bath."

"Let's try something bigger," suggested Prince Fillup. The princes looked around the workroom and spotted something a little bigger than a teaspoon.

"Mother, may we use your good china?" asked Prince MT.

"Just this once," said the queen.

Each boy took a teacup from the royal lunch tray and ran back to the moat. This time they returned with two cups of chilly moat water. They emptied the teacups into the tub.

Splish! Splash!

About how many cups of water do
you think it would take to fill the tub?
About 5? About 50? About 500? More?

14

The king peered into the bathtub. The water hardly covered the bottom of the tub. "At this rate, it will take several days to fill the tub. There must be a better way."

"Father, what if we use those gallon pitchers?" suggested Prince MT. He pointed to two empty crockery pitchers that had once been filled with apple cider from the royal apple orchard.

"One of your mother's best inventions. Try them!" said the king.

The two princes each carried a gallon pitcher to the moat. They filled the pitchers and struggled back with their heavy loads. Then the king and the queen emptied the pitchers into the tub.

WHOOSH! GLUG! GLUG!

Do you think it would take more gallons of water or more cups of water to fill the tub?

The king and queen examined the water in the tub. "Now, that's more like it!" said he.

"If we only had more pitchers, filling the tub would be easy work!" said she.

"There must be a hundred empty pitchers, just like those, in the royal kitchen," Prince MT said.

"We could use those and get everyone to help us," said Prince Fillup.

"Brilliant!" said the queen.

The king and queen summoned all the knights, knaves, squires, pages, cooks, and ladies-in-waiting, and gave them each a pitcher from the kitchen. Each filled his or her pitcher and emptied it into the bathtub. Soon the bathtub was full of icy-cold water from the moat.

16

Using a poker, the king slid a few burning logs from the fireplace to the stone floor under the tub, while the queen worked at her bench. Soon the water was warm and the princes were anxious to take a bath.

"Wait! Before you get in, I have a new invention for you to try," said the queen. She poured a bottle of blue liquid into the steaming water. The water began to froth and foam.

"Wow, Mom! What do you call that?" asked Prince Fillup.

"I think I will call it bubble bath!" said the queen.

The two boys got into their parents' new invention and had the first bubble bath in the kingdom of Math-a-lot.

On her way back to the polka-dot road Alice smelled something delicious. So she crossed the road and followed her nose.

A Piece of Cake

Today was a day of great celebration in Fraction Common. It was Princess Pauline's birthday. The royal baker was making a special cake that the princess herself had ordered. It was to be a round cake about so high and yea big around, an enormous cake for the princess and her guests.

First the royal baker made a crackling fire under the biggest oven in the castle kitchen. Then he began to mix the batter. His recipe called for 30 dozen egg whites, 175 cups of flour, 100 cups of sugar, 50 cups of butter, 50 cups of milk, 50 teaspoons of vanilla, and 200 teaspoons of baking powder! The cake was to be frosted with 7 gallons of the royal baker's secret buttercream frosting, the princess's favorite.

MATH FOCUS: FRACTIONS AND DIVISION READINESS. Children explore the concept of fractions by seeing how a whole cake can be divided into halves, thirds, fourths, and sixths.

Have your child find Fraction Common on the map of Numberland. Help your child understand that the "larger" the fraction word, the smaller the amount: for example, a sixth of a cake is smaller than a third of a cake.

The royal baker poured the batter into the most gigantic cake pan in the land and slid it into the oven. The delicious smell of the baking cake wafted over the castle walls and throughout the kingdom.

When the cake was done, the royal baker took it out of the oven. Just as he smoothed on the last knifeful of frosting, he felt someone breathing hotly down his neck. "That cake smells good. May I have some?"

Startled, the royal baker spun around. It was a dragon! The baker shook like a leaf. "What shall I do?" he thought. "I have to save the kingdom."

"Well?" asked the dragon, breathing out fire and smoke.

The baker could barely speak. "Dear dragon, spare the kingdom and you can have the whole cake."

"Delightful!" exclaimed the dragon.

How many roses are on the cake?

Just as the dragon was about to devour the cake, a griffin landed on the castle wall.

"What smells so good?" she called. "Whatever it is, I want some."

The baker didn't quite know what to do. The dragon had been so agreeable. Maybe he would be willing to split the cake. "Dear dragon, will you share?" quaked the royal baker.

"Yes, we can share. There's enough cake for both of us," said the dragon.

"Very well," said the griffin.

"I'll cut the cake into 2 equal parts, half for you and half for the dragon," said the royal baker. He was just about to cut the cake in half when a gnarly old troll burst into the castle.

How many roses are on each half of the cake?

"Hungry. Want what smells good," grunted the troll.

The royal baker begged the dragon and the griffin, "Could you please share the cake with this troll?"

"Certainly," replied the dragon.

"Why not?" said the griffin.

"OK share. Cake big. Want piece," growled the troll.

"Then I will cut the cake into 3 pieces, equal in size: a third for the dragon, a third for the griffin, and a third for you," said the royal baker.

"Goody, goody," said the troll, licking his chops.

The baker was just about to divide the cake into thirds when the ground began to shake. The baker froze in his tracks. Even the dragon was a bit frightened.

"Fee, fi, fo, fum. I smell a cake baked by someone," bellowed a giant.

"I can't believe this," groaned the baker.

"I'm having a very bad day."

How many roses are on each piece? Which is more, half of the cake or a third of the cake?

If the giant wants cake too, what fraction, or part of the cake, will each visitor get?

"Can I have a piece?" asked the giant. "I love buttercream frosting."

"Certainly," said the dragon. "We will all share the cake."

"Hurry. Cut cake. Starving," bellowed the troll.

"I will cut the cake into 4 pieces, all the same size. I will give a fourth of the cake to the dragon, a fourth to the griffin, a fourth to the troll, and a fourth to the giant."

"That sounds fair," said the giant.

But just as the royal baker was about to cut the cake into fourths, there was a great cheer outside as the princess came out of her chambers and walked across the castle lawn.

The royal baker didn't know what to do. He was afraid the princess would be angry that he was about to give away her specially ordered birthday cake.

How many roses are on each piece?

What happens to the size of the pieces each time someone else wants cake?

"Royal baker, I see you have already met my birthday guests. Is the cake ready?"

"Your *birthday guests*? Your *cake*? Oh, yes, Your Highness. Just as you ordered," said the baker with a sigh of relief.

"Magnificent!" said the princess. "Then let's start the party! Cut a slice for me and for each of my guests and don't forget to cut a slice for yourself as well."

The princess received the presents that her friends had brought, and she gave them party hats and favors.

The baker counted 6 for cake. He held the knife steady and cut the cake into 6 equal-sized pieces: a sixth for the dragon, a sixth for the griffin, a sixth for the troll, a sixth for the giant, a sixth for himself, and a sixth for the birthday girl, Princess Pauline!

How many roses are on each piece?

23

Cut the Cake

1. Get 4 different colors of construction paper. Trace around a plate to make a circle on each piece.

2. Cut out the circles. Decorate each "cake" using crayons or markers.

3. Fold one cake in half. Cut on the fold line.

4. Fold another in half. Fold it in half again to make fourths. Cut on the fold lines.

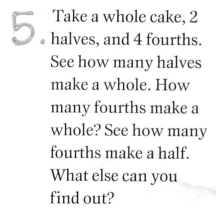

5. Take a whole cake, 2 halves, and 4 fourths. See how many halves make a whole. How many fourths make a whole? See how many fourths make a half. What else can you find out?

MATH FOCUS: FRACTIONS. By cutting out equal parts of a whole, children get hands-on experience with halves, fourths, and eighths, and making equivalent fractions.

Supervise as your child cuts out each circle.

6. Fold the last cake in half.

7. Fold it again to make fourths.

8. Fold it again to make eighths.

9. Cut on the fold lines.

10. See how many eighths make a whole. See how many eighths make a half. How many eighths make a fourth? What else can you find out?

MORE FUN. Your child can challenge family members to make sets of equivalent fractions.

Alice
AND THE
SEVENS

Make the numbers in each loop total **7.**

The opposite sides of a die always add up to 7.
How many dots are on the bottom of this die?
How many dots are on the back?
How many dots are on the right side?

What are the seven days of the week?

We are the 7 continents of the world.

Can you say our names?

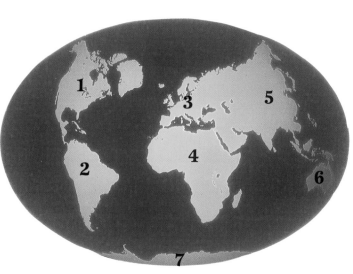

1 North America, **2** South America, **3** Europe, **4** Africa, **5** Asia, **6** Australia, **7** Antarctica

MATH FOCUS: THE CALENDAR, GEOMETRY, MONEY, ADDITION, AND SUBTRACTION. By exploring the number 7 in several different areas of mathematics, children interpret its many uses in the real world.

Have a die available to show your child that the opposite faces always add up to 7.

I am a coin from England. People there call me a 50-pence piece. I'm worth about 90¢. I am the shape of a heptagon. How many sides do I have?

SIETE (see-yet-ay)

Here's how people say me in Spanish.

SEPT (set)

Here's how people say me in French.

SETTE (set-ay)

Here's how people say me in Italian.

How do you say me in English?

How many toothpicks do you need to make 2 squares?

MORE FUN. Your child can make up some riddles involving the number 7 and then challenge family members to solve them.

As she waved to Number Card 7, Alice felt something touch her shoe. She looked down and saw 2 frogs pulling 2 tiny gnomes. "I have to watch this," thought Alice.

The Gnomes Build a Home

Once, in Shape City,
Our story begins,
There lived 2 young gnomes:
Identical twins!

Their clothes were the same
From their toes to their hair.
On Pete's hat was a circle,
On Mike's was a square.

Pete had a frog
With a bow that was red.
Mike had a frog
With a blue bow instead.

MATH FOCUS: PLANE SHAPES, SOLID SHAPES, AND LOGICAL THINKING. By comparing nearly identical pictures, children practice visual problem-solving skills.

Have your child find Shape City on the map of Numberland. Help your child compare each pair of pictures on page 31.

One day Pete decided
He needed a home.
One that was just
The right size for a gnome.

He trudged off to locate
Some building materials.
He found some milk cartons,
And boxes from cereals,

Some paper towel tubes,
And some dried macaroni,
A few cubes of sugar,
And a string from bologna.

Then Pete drew a plan
With ruler and pen.
He planned a gnome home
That he could live in.

He drew rectangular sides
And rectangular doors,
And inside he drew
Square tiles on the floors.

MORE FUN. Your child can construct a "gnome home" with materials found around the house: empty milk cartons, paper towel tubes, macaroni, buttons, spools of thread, etc.

Then one day, Mike came
To see Pete's construction.
And decided to make
His own reproduction.

But Mike didn't follow
Pete's plan precisely.
Can you find Mike's 4 changes,
Which turned out quite nicely?

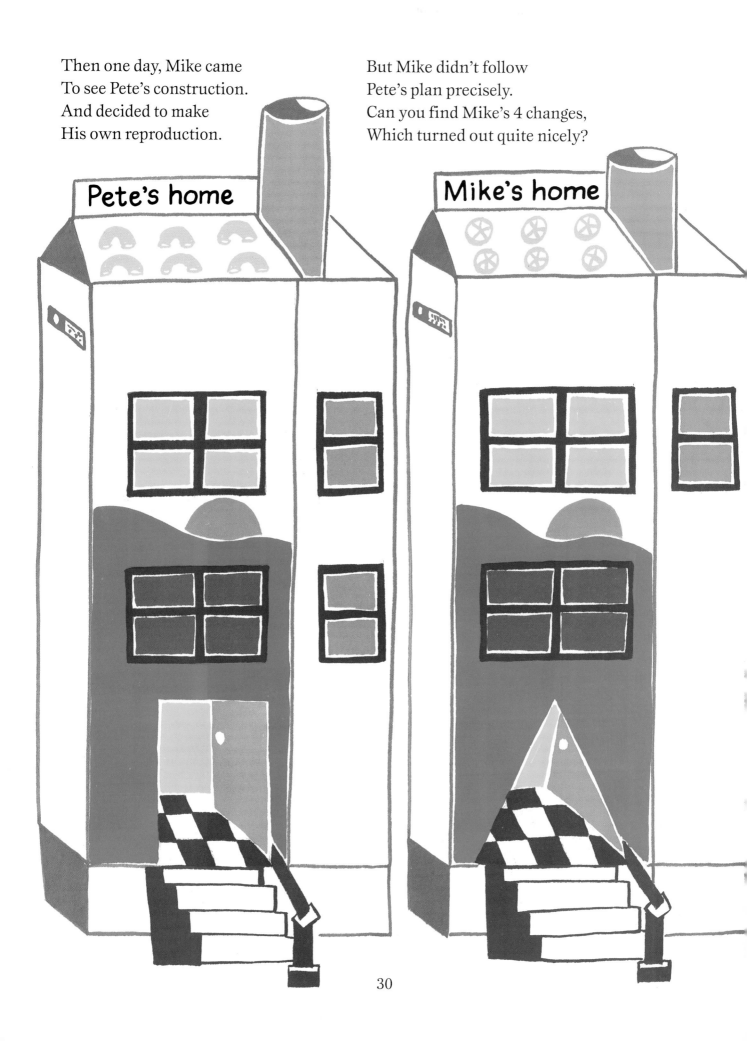

Pete's home

Mike's home

30

In the rooms of each house
Many things are the same.
But some things are different.
Which ones can you name?

Here is Pete's bedroom.
Compare it with Mike's.
What 3 things are different?
They are not alike.

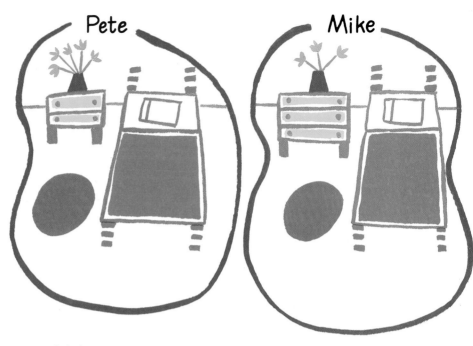

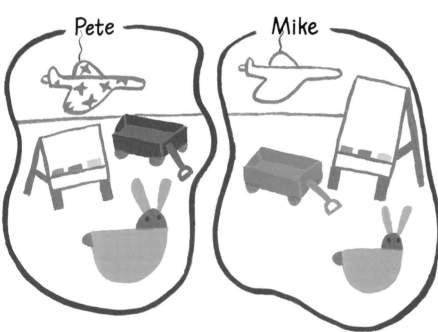

Here are the 2 playrooms
That were built by the boys.
Find 4 things that are different
When you compare all their toys.

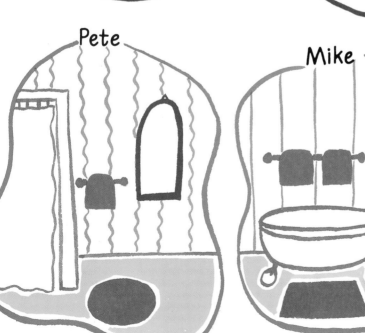

Look at each bathroom
From ceiling to floor.
Can you find 5 differences,
No fewer, no more?

Block Boulevard

"Look!" said Alice. "These buildings are made of blocks called cubes! A cube is a solid with 6 equal square sides."

The hot dog stand was built with 1 cube. The gas station was built with 2 cubes.

Here are the school and the inn. Which building could you make with only 6 cubes?

How many cubes would you need to build the inn?

What color is the cube above the green cube in the inn?

The pizza parlor was built with 4 cubes.

PIZZA

LIBRARY

The library was built with 6 cubes. How many of them can you see?

SHAPE CITY APARTMENTS

ROLLER RINK

FOUR CORNERS MALL

CANDY

ROSIE'S

PEN STATION

GLASSES

How many cubes would you need to build this apartment building? How about the mall?

How many more cubes would you need for the mall than for the apartment building?

What color is the cube next to the yellow cube in the mall?

MORE FUN. Ask your child more questions about Block Boulevard, such as: *What color is the cube between the yellow cube and the green cube in the school? What color is the top cube in the apartment building?*

POPPED PANES

By Royal Decree:

The reader of this scroll is ordered to help Glenda the Glazier repair the broken windows in the castle of Shape City. The windowpanes popped out when a dragon with a terrible cold sneezed! KERCHOO! Look carefully at the overall pattern of each window. Then choose the panes from the border that have the proper shape, size, and color to fit.

Signed,
*King Rightangle III and
Queen Catherine of Hexagon*

MATH FOCUS: PATTERNS, PLANE SHAPES, SYMMETRY, AND SPATIAL SENSE. By analyzing the patterns in stained-glass windows, children identify the sizes, shapes, and colors of the missing panes.

Help your child determine which panes are missing by looking at the pattern of each window. Have your child refer to each shape by its attributes, such as "large red circle," "small blue square," and so on.

Point to the pieces that will fit exactly.
Be sure to consider shape, size, and color.

What shape is this window? Point to all the squares in the window.
Can you find an octagon in the window? How many sides does it have?

MORE FUN. Your child can create his or her own
stained-glass windows by cutting out a variety of
shapes from colored tissue paper and pasting them on
white paper or waxed paper.

Point to the pieces that will fit exactly.
What shape is this window?
Look at the 4 triangles near the middle of the window.
What shape do they make all together?
Find a large rectangle made up of 4 small rectangles.

Point to the pieces that will fit exactly.
What shape is this window?
How many circles are there within the window?
What is the name of the shape in the center of the window?
Can you see a star in the window? What other shapes do you see?

Alice
AND THE
TENS

I look like the letter of the alphabet between W and Y. I am the Roman numeral for 10. What am I?

How many starfish are there?
How many arms does each one have?
How many arms are there in all?

I am a decagon. Each of my sides is the same length. How many sides do I have?

I am a dime. What could you trade me for?

MATH FOCUS: THE CALENDAR, WEIGHT, MONEY, ADDITION, AND SUBTRACTION. By exploring the number 10, children interpret its many uses in the real world.

Have 1 dime, 2 nickels, and 10 pennies available. Ask your child to show 4 different ways to make 10¢.

What number is 3 less than me?
What number is 2 more than me?
What number do you add to 4 to get me?
What number do you subtract from 15 to get me?
Am I an odd or an even number?

I am the month to pick pumpkins.
You may put on a scary costume on my last day.
I am the tenth month of the year.
What month am I?

Which is heavier, a 10-pound bag of
potatoes or a
10-pound bag
of feathers?

FEATHERS
10 POUNDS

POTATOES
10 POUNDS

ten

MORE FUN. Using cereal pieces or dried beans, help
your child count out 30 pieces. Then have your child
put the pieces into groups of 10 each. How many
groups does he or she have?

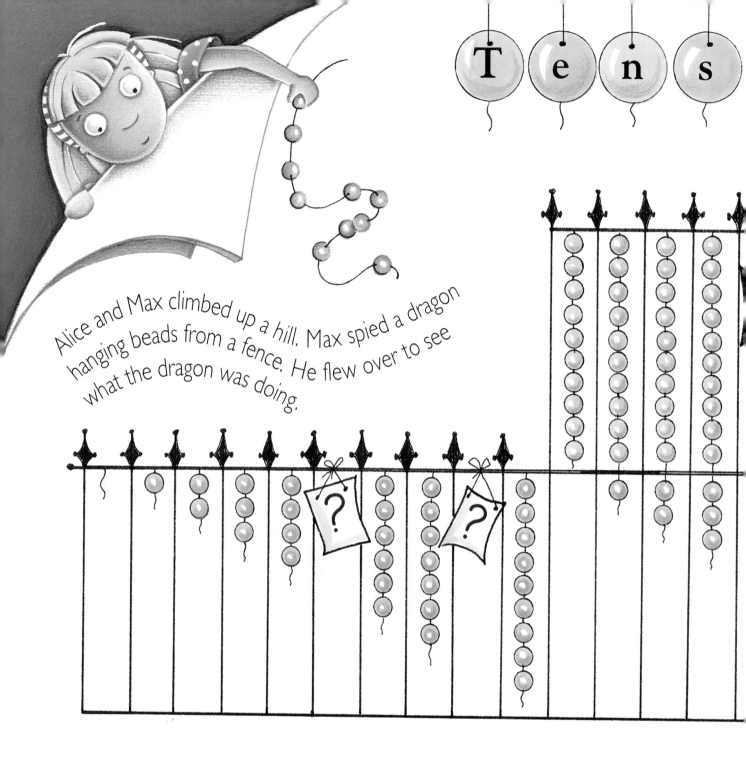

Alice and Max climbed up a hill. Max spied a dragon hanging beads from a fence. He flew over to see what the dragon was doing.

"Hi," said the dragon. "Glad to see you, Max. I've been busy setting up some puzzles. I'll bet you want to do one. Look at the beads. Can you tell what's missing?"

What do you think Max answered?

MATH FOCUS: PLACE VALUE (COUNTING AND GROUPING). By seeing how beads are grouped by tens and ones, children learn the basics of our place-value numeration system.

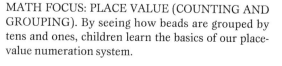

Have your child find Tens Place on the map of Numberland. Your child can count out loud to find the answers to the questions in this story.

Place

Max said, "I see a pattern. It goes 'zero, one, two, three, four,' and I think the next number is 'five,' because it continues 'six, seven.' Then comes 'eight,' then 'nine.'

"I see what you did next. You moved 'ten' up to another fence and continued the pattern, 'eleven, twelve, thirteen.'"

What other numbers are missing?

MORE FUN. Ask your child to say these numbers in the dragon's language: 25, 37, 59, 98. (Answers: two tens plus five, three tens plus seven, five tens plus nine, nine tens plus eight.)

"Eleven, twelve, thirteen?" repeated the dragon. "What strange words! That's not what I say. I say 'one ten plus one, one ten plus two, one ten plus three.' "

"Well," said Max thoughtfully as he wrote numbers on some cards, "I think we are both saying the same thing. In my land, we say 'eleven' for 'one ten plus one,' 'twelve' for 'one ten plus two,' and 'thirteen' for 'one ten plus three.' The missing number is 'one ten plus four' or 'fourteen.' "

How would Max say the number on this fence? How would the dragon say it?

"Here is a Puzzle Fence I made for you," said the dragon. "Can you match the beads on each bar with the number cards?"

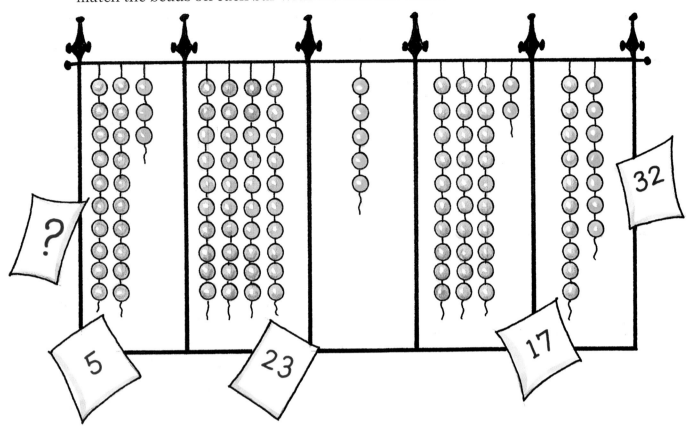

Max decided to make a Puzzle Fence for the dragon. "Now it's your turn," he said. "Can you match the beads with the number cards?"

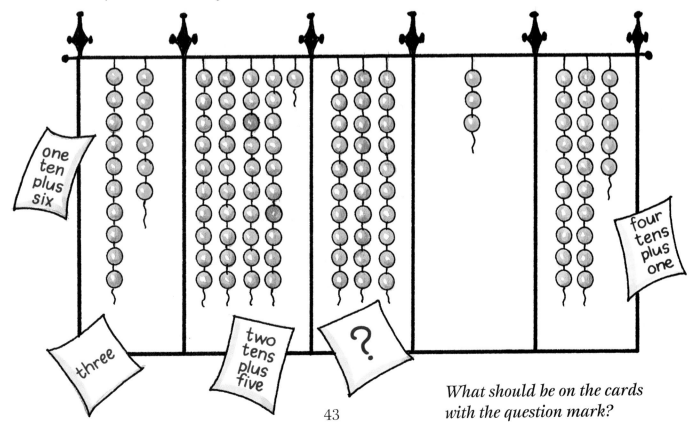

What should be on the cards with the question mark?

Then the dragon showed Max another puzzle. "A stepping-stone path with missing numbers," said Max, "but it stretches so far I can't see all of it."

"Let's rearrange the stones," suggested the dragon. She placed the stones in 5 rows with 10 numbers in each one.

Max looked up and down the rows, to the left and to the right. Soon he saw a pattern. "Now it's easy to name the missing numbers," he said.

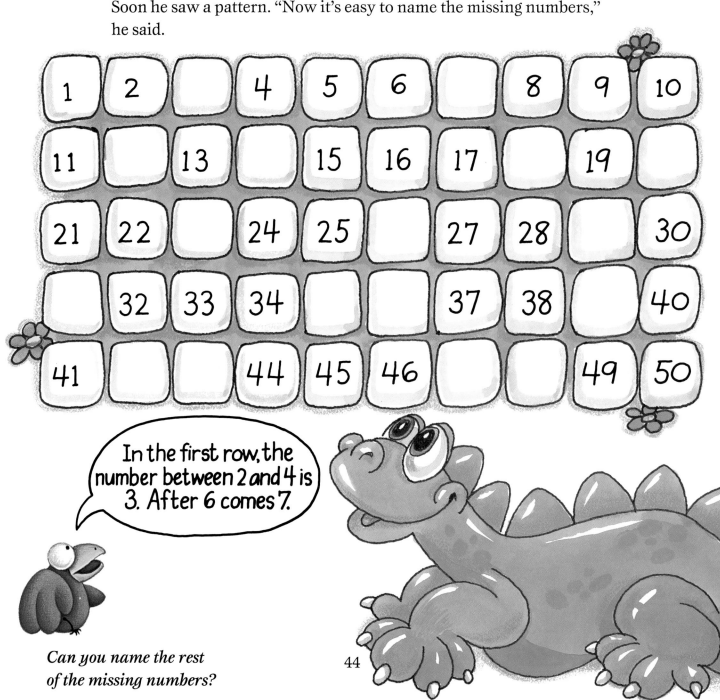

In the first row, the number between 2 and 4 is 3. After 6 comes 7.

Can you name the rest of the missing numbers?

44

Good job, Max!

Max then wrote all the missing numbers on the stones. What patterns can you find as you look at the rows?

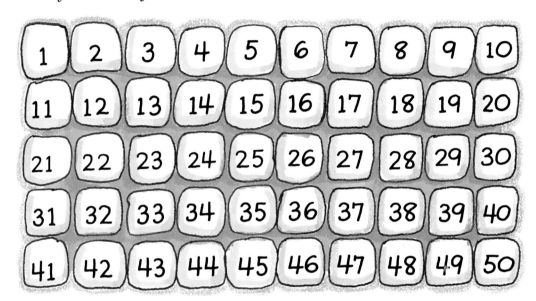

1	2	3	4	5	6	7	8	9	10
11	12	13	14	15	16	17	18	19	20
21	22	23	24	25	26	27	28	29	30
31	32	33	34	35	36	37	38	39	40
41	42	43	44	45	46	47	48	49	50

Here are some stepping stones. What numbers are missing?
Use the stepping-stone chart above to help you.

·ONE MORE PUZZLE·
Put your finger on the largest one-digit number.
Add 10. Subtract 2. Add 10. Subtract 2. Are you on the value of a quarter?

Alice AND THE TWELVES

There are 12 of me in a year. What am I? Which one of me is your birthday in?

I am Izzy the inchworm. How many of me would it take to equal 1 foot?

I am a dodecahedron. I am a solid shape. I have 12 sides, but you can't see all of them here. What shape is each side?

INCHES
0   1   2   3   4   5

MATH FOCUS: THE CALENDAR, TIME, LENGTH, ADDITION, AND SUBTRACTION. By exploring the number 12 in several different areas of mathematics, children think about its many uses in the real world.

August
S M T W T F S

September
S M T W T F S

October
S M T W T F S
1
2 3 4 5 6 7 8
9 10 11 12 13 14 15
16 17 18 19 20 21 22
23 24 25 26 27 28 29
30 31

November
S M T W T F S
1 2 3 4 5
6 7 8 9 10 11 12
13 14 15 16 17 18 19
20 21 22 23 24 25 26
27 28 29 30

December
S M T W T F S
1 2 3
4 5 6 7 8 9 10
11 12 13 14 15 16 17
18 19 20 21 22 23 24
25 26 27 28 29 30 31

When the minute hand and the hour hand point to me during the day it is noon. When the minute hand and the hour hand point to me during the night it is midnight. What number am I?

5	5	2
1	?	?
6	?	3

Numbers in this square add to 12 whether you add down, across, or diagonally. What are the missing numbers?

I am a word that means 12 of something. Eggs are sold by this word. What word am I?

7 8 9 10 11 12

MORE FUN. Have your child count the months of the year. Then have him or her point to the fourth month, the seventh month, and the twelfth month.

47

Alice's Adventures IN SYMBOLVILLE

Alice followed the path through Numberland. She walked through woods where the trees were covered with numbers, and shapes grew like wildflowers. Soon she saw a sign that said "Symbolville."

Welcome to Symbolville!

I'm Alice. Are you math symbol cards?

MATH FOCUS: SIMPLE EQUATIONS, GREATER THAN, LESS THAN. By examining different number sentences, children learn about the equal symbol, and the "greater than" and "less than" symbols.

Have your child find Symbolville on the map of Numberland. Tell your child that the pointed "closed" part of the "less than" (<) and "greater than" (>) symbols always points to the smaller amount.

MORE FUN. Your child can cut out 15 card-size pieces of paper, and on each one write one of the following numbers and symbols: 0, 1, 2, 3, 4, 5, 6, 7, 8, 9, +, −, =, <, >. Then he or she can make the 3 kinds of number sentences shown in the story.

I am a rectangle. I am 8 squares long and 2 squares wide.
How many squares do I have altogether?
How many groups of 2 squares do I have?

Alice
AND THE
SIXTEENS

How many 4-leaf clovers do you see?
How many leaves do they have altogether?

What am I?

I weigh exactly 16 ounces.

MATH FOCUS: WEIGHT, MONEY, AND MULTIPLICATION READINESS. By exploring the number 16 in several different areas of mathematics, children interpret the many uses of numbers encountered in the real world.

Have available 1 dime, 3 nickels, and 16 pennies. Have your child show how to make 16¢ in 4 different ways.

I am a square.
How many groups of 4 little squares do I have?

What number do you double to get me?
I have 1 ten. How many ones do I have?
Am I greater than or less than the number
of fingers *and* toes you have?
How many ways can you make 16?

16

How can you make 16¢ . . .
with 3 coins?
with 4 coins?
with 7 coins?

I know that!

What is the sixteenth letter of the alphabet?

16

MORE FUN. Your child can make up some riddles involving the number 16 and challenge family members to solve them.

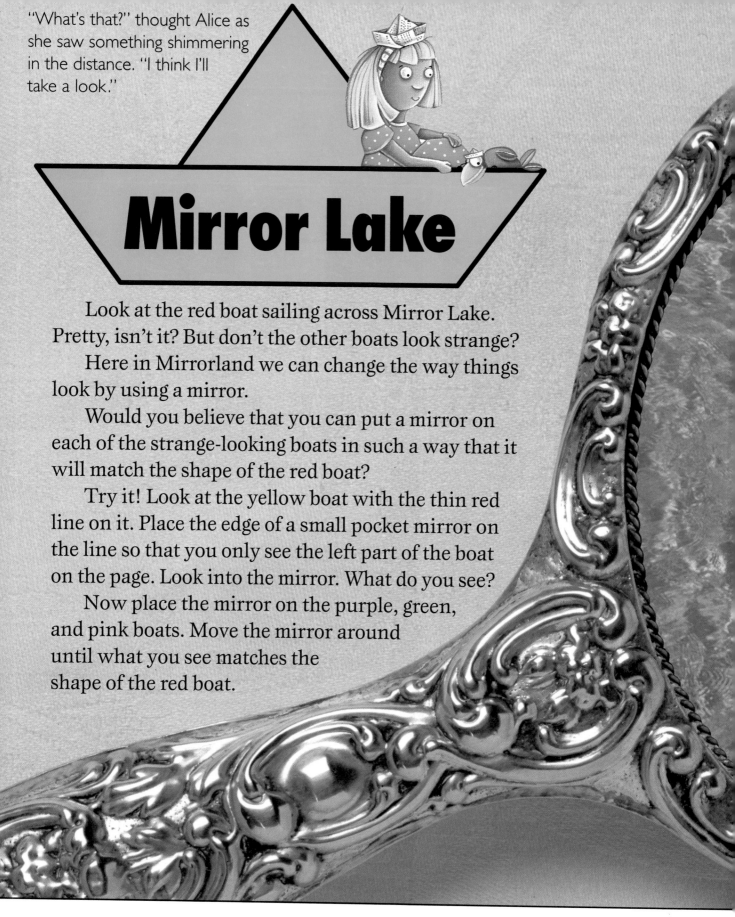

"What's that?" thought Alice as she saw something shimmering in the distance. "I think I'll take a look."

Mirror Lake

Look at the red boat sailing across Mirror Lake. Pretty, isn't it? But don't the other boats look strange?

Here in Mirrorland we can change the way things look by using a mirror.

Would you believe that you can put a mirror on each of the strange-looking boats in such a way that it will match the shape of the red boat?

Try it! Look at the yellow boat with the thin red line on it. Place the edge of a small pocket mirror on the line so that you only see the left part of the boat on the page. Look into the mirror. What do you see?

Now place the mirror on the purple, green, and pink boats. Move the mirror around until what you see matches the shape of the red boat.

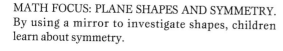

MORE FUN. Your child can challenge family
members to solve these mirror puzzles.

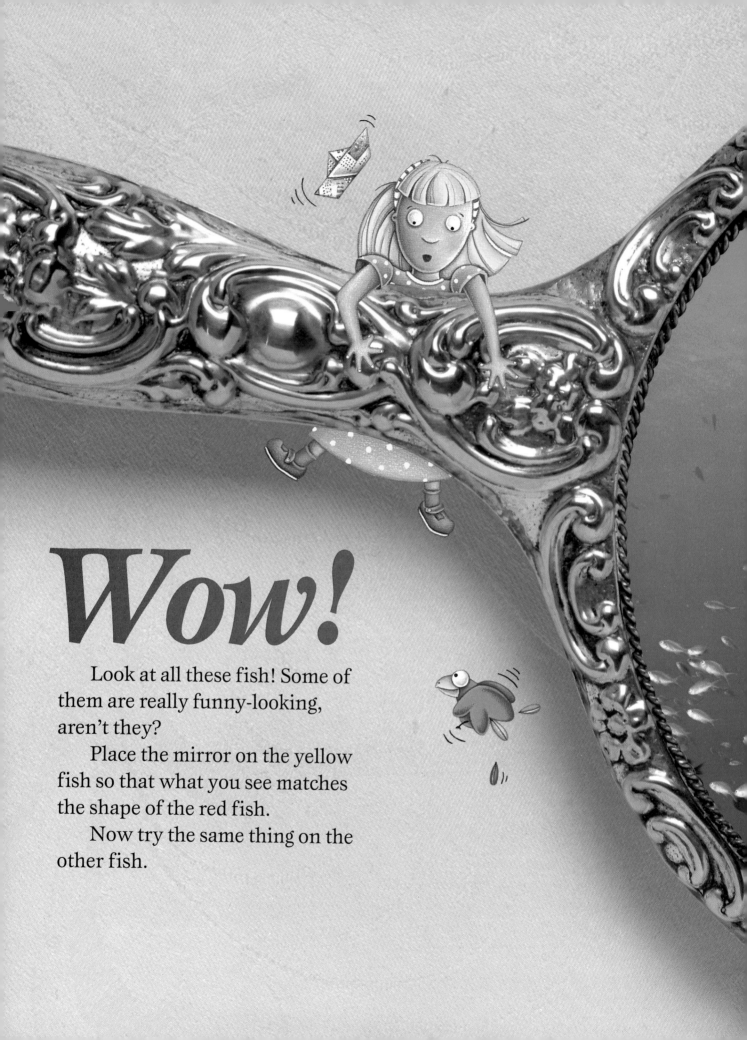

Wow!

Look at all these fish! Some of them are really funny-looking, aren't they?

Place the mirror on the yellow fish so that what you see matches the shape of the red fish.

Now try the same thing on the other fish.

"My, what a little riddle rabbit," said Alice as she knelt down to pick it up.

"Yes," said Number Card 21, "but this little rabbit has a very big riddle. Here, this magnifying glass will help you read it."

"Thank you," said Alice. "I see, it's a number sentence. It's a long number sentence. It's a very, very long number sentence. But it isn't finished."

"That's the problem," said the number card. "When you finish this number sentence you can find your way home."

"But I can't do this in my head," wailed Alice. "Listen, I'll read it to you:
$$1 + 2 + 156 - 5 + 27 + 3 - 120 + 77 + 400 - 2 + 17 - 535 = \boxed{?}$$"

"Well, that's your riddle, and your problem," said the number card. "I'll leave you to find the solution. Call me when you're ready."

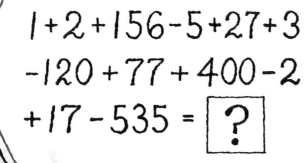

$$1 + 2 + 156 - 5 + 27 + 3$$
$$-120 + 77 + 400 - 2$$
$$+ 17 - 535 = \boxed{?}$$

MATH FOCUS: ADDITION AND SUBTRACTION OF LARGER NUMBERS. By using a calculator to solve a complicated number sentence, children add and subtract larger numbers. Your child can cover a number with a penny as he or she enters it into the calculator.

"Call," thought Alice. "I'll call for help! That's what I'll do." Alice went into the phone booth and dialed 555-MEOW.

"Hello," said a sleepy voice. "Professor Guesser here. No problem too big, no problem too small. How can I help you?"

"Oh, Professor, it's Alice," she replied. "I'm in trouble. I'm in Numberland and I must solve a very long number problem before suppertime. Can you help me? I'm with Number Card 21, just past Mirror Lake."

"Of course I'll help. I was just taking a little catnap. Don't worry. I'll get dressed and be there in two shakes of a kitten's tail. I know the polka-dot road like the back of my paw. See you soon."

How might Professor Guesser help Alice?

What numbers would you dial for Professor Guesser's phone number?

MORE FUN. Ask your child to solve these 2 number sentences on the calculator: $5 + 126 - 90 + 3 + 7 + 463 - 101 + 61 - 3 - 299 + 80 - 126 - 83 + 1 + 10 - 8 - 25 = ?$ and $30 + 1 - 5 + 190 + 72 - 23 - 44 + 362 - 8$

$- 2 + 112 - 30 + 4 - 333 + 87 + 568 - 107 + 2 - 855 = ?$ (The answer for both is 21.) Your child can also create his or her own number sentence with an answer of 21.

Before she left, Professor Guesser put a small, flat object in her coat pocket and made an adjustment to her motorcycle. Then she whizzed onto the highway and followed the signs to Numberland.

EXIT 21
NUMBERLAND
POLKA DOT ROAD
NEXT RIGHT

What do you think the small, flat object might be?

$$1 + 2 + 156 - 5 + 27 + 3 - 120 + 77 + 400 - 2 + 17 - 535 = \boxed{?}$$

"Hello, Alice," said Professor Guesser. "Let me have a look at your riddle. Have you tried to solve it while you were waiting for me?"

"Oh, yes," said Alice. "But when I get partway through, I forget where I am and I have to start all over again."

"That happens to almost everybody. Very few people can do such long number sentences in their heads. A good strategy is to use this." Professor Guesser handed Alice the small, flat object. "It's yours to keep."

"A calculator!" exclaimed Alice. "Why didn't I think of that?"

"You will next time," said Professor Guesser. "Now you can complete that number sentence while I tell the number card you're ready to go."

Alice had the answer in about a minute.

"That's correct," said Number Card 21. "You are a clever girl. Now you can get home in time for supper, just as you wanted."

"I wouldn't have solved my problem in time without your help, Professor Guesser," Alice said gratefully. "You're amazing!"

"If you think I'm amazing," replied Professor Guesser, "just wait till you see the road home!"

63

Use your calculator to help Alice find the answer.

TIME-LIFE for CHILDREN®

Publisher: Robert H. Smith
Associate Publisher and Managing Editor: Neil Kagan
Assistant Managing Editor: Patricia Daniels
Editorial Directors: Jean Burke Crawford, Allan Fallow,
    Karin Kinney, Sara Mark, Elizabeth Ward
Director of Marketing: Margaret Mooney
Product Managers: Cassandra Ford,
    Shelley L. Schimkus
Director of Finance: Lisa Peterson
Financial Analyst: Patricia Vanderslice
Administrative Assistant: Barbara A. Jones
Production Manager: Marlene Zack
Production: Celia Beattie
Supervisor of Quality Control: James King
Assistant Supervisor of Quality Control: Miriam Newton

Produced by Kirchoff/Wohlberg, Inc.
866 United Nations Plaza
New York, New York 10017

Series Director: Mary Jane Martin
Creative Director: Morris A. Kirchoff
Mathematics Director: Jo Dennis
Designers: Jessica A. Kirchoff, Daniel Moreton
Assistant Designers: Brian Collins, Judith Schwartz
Contributing Writers: Gloria Armstrong, Anne M. Miranda
Managing Editor: Nancy Pernick
Editors: Susan M. Darwin, Beth Grout, David McCoy

Cover Illustration: Daniel Moreton

Illustration Credits: Lizi Boyd, pp. 28–31; Liz Callen, pp. 9,
12–17; Susan M. Darwin, pp. 32–33; Ron LeHew, pp. 40–45;
Tom Leonard, p. 10; Anne M. Miranda, pp. 34–37; Don Madden,
pp. 60–63, back end papers; Daniel Moreton, end papers, pp. 6–9,
48–53, 60–63; Troy Viss, pp. 10–11, 26–27, 38–39, 46–47, 54–55;
Viki Woodworth, pp. 18–25.

All Alice and Max spots: Daniel Moreton

First printing. Printed in U.S.A.
Published simultaneously in Canada.

Time Life Inc. is a wholly owned subsidary of THE TIME INC.
BOOK COMPANY

TIME-LIFE is a trademark of Time Warner Inc. U.S.A.

For subscription information, call 1-800-621-7026.

CONSULTANTS

Mary Jane Martin spent 17 years working in elementary
school classrooms as a teacher and reading consultant; for
seven of those years she was a first-grade teacher. The second
half of her career has been devoted to publishing. During this
time she has helped create and produce a wide variety of
innovative elementary programs, including two mathematics
textbook series.

Jo Dennis has worked as a teacher and math consultant in
England, Australia, and the United States for more than 20
years. Most recently, she has helped develop and write several
mathematics textbooks for kindergarten, first grade, and
second grade.

Catherine Motz Peterson is a curriculum specialist
who spent five years developing an early elementary
mathematics program for the nationally acclaimed Fairfax
County Public Schools in Virginia. She is also mathematics
consultant to the University Of Maryland, Catholic
University, and the Fredrick County Public Schools in
Maryland. Ms. Peterson is the director of the Capitol Hill
Day School in Washington, D.C.

Photography Credits: Pages 10, 24–25(bkgd.), 27(b), 38, 46,
47, 55, 56–59, Justin Kirchoff; 26, Terje Kveen, The Image
Bank; 56–57(inset), Tony Stone Images; 58–59(inset), Fred
McConnaughey, Photo Researchers.

Library of Congress Cataloging-in-Publication Data
Alice in numberland : fantasy math.
        p.   cm. – (I love math)
        Summary: A collection of stories, poems, riddles,
games, and hands-on activities reflecting Alice's adventures in
Numberland, where she finds mathematical challenges
throughout the magical landscape.
        ISBN 0-8094-9978-9
        1. Mathematics–Juvenile literature. [1. Mathematics.
2. Mathematical recreations.] I. Time-Life for Children (Firm)
II. Series.
QA40.5.A45   1993
510–dc20   93-9136
                                                         CIP
                                                          AC

AMAZING
Alice

Help Alice and Professor Guesser find their way through the maze. They want to get home before their supper gets cold.

START HERE